# The right side of the hedge

Country Life Today

Well, Mister Someone, these people come down here and take us all to be fools. They come here to forget what they've created elsewhere and do exactly the same. They can keep their money and their fancy ways. I believe I'm living on the right side of the hedge, and no one can tell me different.

# The right side of the hedge

## Country Life Today

# Chris Chapman

## Introduction by Ian Niall

**David & Charles**
Newton Abbot · London · Vancouver · North Pomfret (VT)

ISBN 0 7153 7342 0

Library of Congress Catalog Card Number 77-89372

© Chris Chapman 1977
  Ian Niall 1977

Set in Monotype 9d on 12pt Univers 685 series
by HBM Typesetting Limited
Standish Street Chorley Lancashire
and printed in Great Britain
by the Alden Press Oxford
for David & Charles (Holdings) Limited
Brunel House Newton Abbot Devon

Published in the United States of America
by David & Charles Inc
North Pomfret Vermont 05053 USA

Published in Canada
by Douglas David & Charles Limited
1875 Welch Street North Vancouver BC

# Contents

*To Tavy, my godson*

# Preface

Since its invention in 1839, photography has stumbled through many phases, today's vogue relying on new gimmicks with more emphasis on what can be achieved in the darkroom than in the actual picture-taking. But photography in its simplest form has more magic than any of these techniques could wish to offer. The camera has the unique ability to capture a moment which can speak of the occasion, with pictures that delight, amuse and sometimes even sadden.

Learning to use the camera can be a painful business. There are no strict rules, but perhaps there are guidelines. It is a myth to suppose that the most expensive will produce the best pictures. In the early part of this century, Jacques Henri-Lartigue, as a mere boy, produced some outstanding pictures of life in France on a simple wooden camera. His pictures speak not of technique, but of a love and understanding of what went on around him.

The camera should really be regarded as a tool, to be mastered and then used to make a photograph. Taking pictures isn't to do with the gleam of modern equipment, or covering mistakes with clever practices; it requires honesty, self-discipline, and a great deal of patience. It is my conviction that if you have this, and keep shooting, you eventually learn.

Chris Chapman,
Dartmoor, 1977

# Introduction

The countryside is everything to those who would live in it. We all have our cherished remembrance or our fond fantasy. It is understandable that when the dream takes over, a curlew calls on the moors of Devon or Cornwall: there is a wavering white surf along the endless rocky coast, slow-moving, high, white cloud to make creeping shadows on the green fells of Cumbria, and smoke eternally curling from the chimneys of thatched cottages tucked away in the New Forest. It doesn't rain on the windy hills of the Cotswolds: the sun always shines on warm Cotswold stone, even when we have a slight distaste for the over-tidiness of the 'tea-and-buttered scone', too perfect village of Broadway. In truth, though daffodils nod in the breeze in Lakeland, it rains there rather a lot. It rains too, on Wenlock Edge, though Mary Webb didn't say too much about it. Sometimes, walking down an English lane a foul odour of slurry meets us rather than the scent of honeysuckle. We don't talk of such things but the man who lives and works in the country isn't sentimental about it, and dreams are what keep the visitor coming. In any case, reality of this sort, insistence upon the stark truth, makes the years lie more heavily on our backs. We don't need to be reminded of the harshness of life. Hogarth may have drawn wrinkles and a wart or two, but most people prefer Constable and Turner: they please the romantic in us and we can walk into their pictures with the wonder of Alice going through the looking glass.

Landscape is always the background to life. As we look down the canyons between high rise rookeries, where office blocks or great lumps of masonry like Battersea Power Station intrude upon our view, we dream of the cool ridges of limestone in North Yorkshire or the birch plantings that are the only topographical feature of the wide horizon on the fens. When we use the word 'timeless' about some of these places we may occasionally be in error. The picture changes, if not month by month and season by season, decade by decade. All our living is against this changing background or the sweet indulgence of nostalgia would surely be less enjoyable. There are few of us who don't suffer from this harmless complaint and would turn the clock back to see again the flock of sheep bundling through a village that is a village no more, their grazing divided by a new motorway, or swifts like black missiles above a farmstead now demolished.

I have spent almost half my life portraying the countryside — that permanent yet evolving background against which the countryman earns his living. Time has impressed upon me the ephemeral nature of what I have been trying to record. There are dramatic changes when long-striding, wide-armed pylons carry cables over hill and dale and cooling towers like gigantic beakers are set down on salt marshes where once duck and waders came and went in peace. Out in the flat country the monster combine crawls steadily along, flailing and felling the wheat or barley, leaving a tousled debris of straw to be burned or hammered into bales. The hayfield, once a place of frantic human activity with rake and fork — and fronds of bracken to drive away the flies — is in the eye of the hurricane where the green forager blows the freshly cut grass into a great container, to be gusted up into a silage tower that dominates the landscape for miles. There is no longer a ploughteam behind which the ploughman limps along. All this is gone as the tractor drones up and down the field and the operator only looks once in a while at the multiple furrows he is making.

There are two things a writer must accept in these circumstances. He must be content to portray what he sees, knowing that it will be old-fashioned and possibly obsolete in a decade and he must recognize the present day countryman for what he is, a quite unsentimental, hastening being with no time to chew on a straw and hang on the gate. Much the same factors apply to the photographer who would make a record of country scenes and country people. He captures a very brief period in time and the way things happen to be in a given season. With changing techniques in such farming activities as animal management and cropping the man with even the most sophisticated camera can't hope to do more than his Victorian grandfather did: he can change nothing except the viewpoint and the clock will only run clockwise. My introduction to this book of pictures of the British countryside is an attempt to interpret what the photographer is saying without putting detailed captions on his work, which would be invidious.

There is nothing easier for a reasonably skilled photographer than the taking of pretty pictures. With the whole of the countryside to choose from, Chris Chapman would have had no difficulty in doing this. He is much more than a reasonably skilled photographer however, and he wouldn't have settled for pretty pictures even if his publisher would have accepted them. He was, in fact, looking for his own kind of truth. When he looked at the landscape he saw the street of a rather grim close-built village, drystone walls radiating from a moorland farm, a caravan of the twentieth-century travelling people with that suggestion of wall-to-wall squalor that a much-used, modern caravan well past its prime can convey. Chris Chapman is no sentimentalist: he stopped to take a picture of these travellers and found himself press-ganged into helping repair their broken-down car. He saw an inhabited Nissen hut not as a scar on the landscape but as much a part of it as Cromwell's warts and, moreover, a place in which people lived and had their being just as much as those who live in fine mansions. Talking to Chris I was able to understand how well he has succeeded in getting to the elements of country life. He knows the simple countrywoman's cherished ornaments and heirlooms, which are certain to be pot and not porcelain, copper and pewter and hardly ever silver. His child at the sink having its head dried with a rough towel is reality he has personally experienced. There is a kind of compassion for the coal-picker on a slag heap that is part of a land-scape once all green fields.

It depends where a man chooses to stand to take his picture, and even so, the camera may lie. Everyone knows its lies from the television advertisement suggesting cool clear streams and tar oil, breakfast cereals processed a half century away from that horse binder and the old way of ploughing. This young photographer's angles and viewpoints tell a great deal about his chosen subjects, but if he took the pictures over again they would tell a slightly different story. Moods change. Old men age and die. The sunlight on a wall is never quite the same and a galloping horse covers different ground. The expression on the rider's face also changes so that the moment is distinct from all others past or to come, for on a second attempt the shutter will close on a different image.

What Chris Chapman really achieves in this selection of photographs is a stimulation of the imagination. He evokes something not in the picture — the smell of burning car tyres round the caravan, an out-of-sight old banger of a car with rusty wings and hanging bumpers shedding chrome. His hunting scenes convey the yelping of hounds, the crack of a whip, the creak of saddle leather and the 'abdominal resonance' that comes as a horse completes a jump. Chris came on the hunting scene with an open mind. He might have expected the blooding ritual but he found instead the terrier man and a different ritual involving a pistol carried in a special wooden case — in the case too, a single round of ammunition for the coup de grace. He knew very little about the hunter and perhaps not a lot more about the fox, but he discovered that both are involved in the life of the countryside. A great gulf lies between those who hunt and those who would impose a restriction on something they see as barbaric, but a photographer need only be a moralist when he sets out to be one. This particular photographer didn't choose to be one. He looked into his viewfinder and saw the hunt and the hounds, a brilliant view. He also saw a wheelwright at work, a shoesmith trimming the hoof of a horse. He saw two typical countrymen standing straddle-legged in conversation at a farm sale, boys snoozing in the shade, an angler playing a salmon that bent his rod in a gentle arc.

Not everyone who looks at Chris Chapman's remarkable set of pictures will see his point of view in every one. That would be too much to hope for, and perhaps impossible. A photographer takes pictures to communicate and communication is always limited, even though the man with the camera may use tricks of his trade. Whether the person who looks at the results of this kind of work really understands what has been done, or appreciates what has been discarded in producing the final collection doesn't matter. What does matter is the total effect of images conveyed in a particular way.

It is, of course, impossible to define what may be called the country landscape or the life of the countryman, for the vistas are endless and the countryman has many occupations. There is no place to begin and no point at which the task may be said to be complete. There will always be other scenes with other players, different casts and other aspects of life to be shown. A photographer must stop somewhere and come out of his darkroom with the final print, saying he has decided to stop here. In spite of this present selection, Chris Chapman probably draws no line. He knows as well as anyone that there is no end to it and I suspect he will go on taking pictures of the background to life in the country until he is an old man. An artist always has a basic inspiration and this, I feel, is his.

Taking pictures isn't necessarily dedication to the beautiful or to the stark and ugly but may be to the character and nature of existence. It is asking a great deal to expect pictures to speak for themselves without a single word from the photographer, but a painter doesn't describe his scene in words and this is what Chris Chapman studied before he took to photography. He really doesn't want to be a writer offering pictures. He has happily agreed to my saying a word for him and about him. Perhaps the most significant thing I can say is that I wish I had taken his pictures, or had the same talent.

Ian Niall,
Llandudno, 1977

'When the dream takes over . . .' the serenity of early morning on an estuary

What would have been a derelict Nissen hut of cracked grey asbestos, became an attractive cottage for Mr and Mrs Ernie Worth. They lived there for some thirty years, the building was demolished recently, condemned by conservationists as a blot on the landscape

'I'm living on the right side of the hedge, and no one can tell me different.' Ernie and Elsie Worth inside the cottage

The rugged beauty of a waterfall above
White Coppice in the Pennines

Contrast of coalmining scars and the
green hillside of a typical Welsh valley.
Here a retired miner helps himself to the
pickings found in the slag heap

Pain before pleasure; a farmer gives
his complaining son a scrub up before
putting in an appearance at the village
carnival

Grubby and wary, a gypsy boy stands his ground before the camera

Travelling people come to rest on a byway near Pendle Hill, Lancashire

The field lost – and the hunt long gone.
A lady comes cantering in search of
huntsmen and pack

In full gallop the tail end of the field
strings out, pursuing a fox which had
continually circled the woods

The terrier man triumphantly holds up
the kill

Holidaymakers from the other side of
the stream

# The Village

Why the village is where it is, the size it is and, equally important, how it remains a centre of population, always intrigues the researcher in history or the geographer concerned with the features of a landscape. The English village is as impossible to describe as the perfume of the tearose. It is not to be classified as typical of the country but rather of the county. Even so, one village in Sussex say, or Hampshire is never exactly like another. This village grew and flourished where it is for some specified reason, while the next one, a few miles along the lane had an entirely different reason for developing there. Time and circumstance have destroyed and restored small settlements down through history. What was recorded in the Domesday book wasn't the last word by a thousand years.

The village is built of warm red brick because there was a claybed within carting distance, or of yellow stone because there was a quarry. The chalk land of the south yielded flint and the grim mountains of the north provided granite or slate. The village grew around the church and the graveyard, the crossroads or the junction of streams where a mill might be turned by the water. It draped itself over a hill because it was a lookout or a good spot for building of the windmill. It huddled in the forest and the charcoal burners and hurdle-makers worked away quietly there. It grew like the oak tree or the beech. It was stunted by the hard winters and sprouted fresh leaves in good years – and it was unplanned. It was created by the needs of people, with no planners nor architects to guide them, but only thatchers and wallers, builders in brick and stone, slaters and tilers making houses and workplaces for millers, bakers, tanners, wheelwrights and smiths. Almost everything that was built was constructed of material close to hand, the oak tree, the boulders from the bed of the stream, lime mortar from the kiln, clay daub and wattle, plaster bonded with horsehair, beams dressed with the adze.

Planners who contemplate the problems of buildings huddling against one another, winding streets, irregular building lines and no damp courses, must sigh to think that their orderly-minded, bureaucratic profession took so long to gain recognition. There would have been none of this eccentricity and expediency had there been *planners* to lay out the village ! They would undoubtedly have insisted upon the grid system. The whole of Britain would have been parcelled into real estate lots. The roads would have delighted the cartographer for they would have run north and south and east and west. All would have been right angles and boxes and we might have anticipated America and named our avenues and numbered our streets. There would have been something else even more 'beneficial' to the public in general had this been possible. People could have been moved about from one end of the country so much more easily. There would have been room for juggernauts in every village street. The villages could all have been gradually upgraded to garden cities when their populations reached a certain figure. The village pond would have been drained and filled in, or surrounded by precast flags and planted with the right waterplants.

Perhaps the only kind of village that would have escaped renovation or planning would have been our long street with the Wild West atmosphere, for this kind of settlement must surely please the present day planner. It grew that way of necessity and hard times, of course, as all villages develop. The long street, wide enough to be remarked upon, came about because it was the habit of commoners to herd in their cattle when plundering invaders ravaged the countryside. The ends of the street could be barricaded or closed off. Within the enclosure pigs hobnobbed with sheep, cattle and horses drank at the pond. The midden grew and flies were a nuisance, but people were used to nuisance and things decomposing in a day when kites perched on the roof to drop down for offal, and dogs ran wild.

Growing through the centuries, the modern village has acquired its character from the fashion of building in one generation overlaying that employed in one past. What it once was may not be recorded in a book, but the names of its streets and buildings hold a clue – Cloth Hall, Sheep Street, Orchard Lane, Mill Road. What survives is what the place needs. It needed the village green and the meeting place. It needed the church and the chapel, the post office in its day, and the police office when the constabulary became a charge on those who paid taxes. It didn't need the village pump or the well at the end of Well Street. It got rid of the soil cart in an enlightened age in which even the villagers could be convinced that in well water and the cesspit lay the road to the graveyard taken by so many of the previous generation at ages so often recorded in single figures.

The modern village has piped water. Its domestic oil lamps are in the window of the antique shop in the nearest town, along with the warming pan, the old brass fender and even the iron cooking pot. The immunized population doesn't die of diphtheria or polio and cooks by electricity, sleeping under an electric blanket or, that continental innovation, the duvet. The field in which the geese grazed is a car park that may lie empty for most of the day, but is sometimes packed with cars when there is some social occasion to draw in the country folk from round about. The church and the pub, rarely very far apart, gather in the righteous and the unrighteous. On the village green there is sometimes cricket on Saturday and Sunday.

Almost invariably the old and the new flank one another as the local authority recognizes the need for more houses. The new places are often set at complementary angles and have alternating paintwork schemes. No one can expect more. The building line won't allow an over-hanging dormer window, a porch or a window that gives the passing villager a view of old grandad steeping his feet before the fire. Cars obstruct the street day and night.

At night the place sleeps. The church clock tolls the passing hours while people sit under their individual television aerials, watching to see whether they are getting the things from life that even a country person is entitled to, a do-it-yourself double-glazing kit, a deep freeze or access to the supermarket. The modern store is as breath-taking as Aladdin's cave and stocked to the ceiling with everything anyone could ever long for – and a lot of things most people would be as well without.

Yet each village still lives and breathes its individual character. Its people are partisan. Long ago the community was always feuding with the people down along the way or over the hill. Everyone knows what the people there are like! How could they be anything else, living in such a miserable place? The village over the hill has a population that commutes to the creamery and the cheese factory. It had no reason for being until its men found work in that factory, but then very few villages are able to support their working population. The village shop could never get by without the rural community coming in for the odd pound of tea or bag of sugar and small items needed before the weekly excursion to the supermarket.

Everyone is aware of the trend: the decline in population due to lack of work, the increase in incomers renovating old cottages for their retirement – weekenders trying to ingratiate themselves and become accepted. The planners have it their way now, of course, and take the dog-leg out of the street, make a layby of what was a turn in the lane, insist upon the signs being coloured green and grudgingly allow the yard at the side of the pub to be used as a car park. The village may be in the process of becoming a town one day!

Change is what every community, large or small undergoes whether its members are aware of it or not. More often in the case of old villages the process is a slow one. The community adapts to a process of decline, accepting that things are not what they were and the world is hurrying by. The most zealous of planners must recognize that what made the heart beat in the eighteenth and nineteenth century isn't there any more. The older generation can't commute and lack the skills to attract new industry so the village remains largely unchanged in appearance. People from the town, already disturbed by the pace of landscaping and development in their own community look at the old village, finding something solid and secure in its stone walls and heavy timbers, its joggled kerbs and uneven flagstones, its belfried church with its yew trees. Here, in their imagination, they conjure up history and see a man in a smock wearing a yoke on which he carries water from the well or a grim-faced Puritan walking the street with his Bible in his folded hand. The dusty corners of the old place hark back to the world that once was when the stocks stood on the square and proclamations were made after the ringing of the bell.

The village that thrives because of a change in the transport system in a particular part of the world, the building of a motorway or a by-pass, absorbs a little of the local farmers' land and grows a bright cluster of modern detached houses that contrast with the old cottages

Without hand signals, village kids try out their new-found barrow

Sheltering walls with open moorland beyond

a few yards down the road. Renovators renovate and improvers improve, and here and there the old people nod their approval. It needed to be changed, they say. It was time it was done for there was nothing for the young people. A village is, after all, the people who live in it. It may be fascinating to look down the well or see the horseshoes nailed to the door of the derelict smithy but relics are not what living is about. People who have to make a living can't afford to be sentimental about things and must weigh up the advantages of the new way. No one would go back to the world the way it was when it was really the world of the workhouse, the poor law and epidemics that had to be put down to the will of God. Perhaps the only drawback to the process of change is that it can never be regulated to suit everyone.

The alternative way is decline. When a village goes into decline, its physicians stop prescribing. It sits there growing old. The planners have their eye on the area. One day they will bulldoze right through it and use the stones to fill holes in the road or buttress a hill against a possible landslide. The place becomes a name on the map. No one goes there. The old people who knew it die and are buried. This happens or begins to happen more frequently than a place expands. When villages are far out they die. When they are close to larger centres of population they are absorbed, as farms are swallowed up or even surrounded by council house estates.

Once in a while a growing number of well-to-do commuters saves the day by settling, one after another, renovating a few of the better old cottages, building new, split-level, centrally-heated houses that change the whole character of the village. Such villages acquire a new look, a different character. The old villagers keep themselves to themselves. The rates go up. The pub serves dinner in a candle-lit annex. The new villager ornaments his front lawn with a couple of stack staddles and a show-piece dogcart or butterchurn. Occasionally he brings a Victorian gaslamp or finds a piece of expensive wrought ironwork made by a Spanish blacksmith. The net result is a village that never was and never will be, and a very sad place indeed, for it is really akin to a bee colony that dwindles and is fed with sugar. There is no substitute for nectar and pollen. Atmosphere is intrinsic, healthy or unhealthy, and the faded adverts at the back of the village shop testify to the fact that once upon a time people asked for no more than 'Bovril to cure a chill', Wild Woodbines for the perfect smoke, and Blackamoor tea to drink. It won't do any more because people believe something else — that big is best, and time is money. The world is contracting and people have no time for the old-fashioned village, the old-fashioned villager and his deadly idea of entertainment.

Crowds assemble on the village green to celebrate a ritual but one old inhabitant gazes suspiciously on the newcomers, many of whom have travelled long distances by car to watch the sport

The sturdy granite walls of this thatched farmhouse have stood since 1656. This man was born here, as were his father and grandfather before him

Two views inside the farmhouse: collecting things, not just antiques but objects with sentimental associations, has always been important to the cottager who knows that a chiming clock, a copper kettle and a piece of pottery can add warmth to a simple room. Fussiness might be the verdict of the townsman looking in on an old chiffonier crammed with treasured pictures, jugs and ornaments, but all these objects represent people, events, and emotions to their proud owners

'The alternative way is decline . . .' an abandoned farmhouse. As with so many uninhabited buildings, the vegetation has slowly begun to take over

The demands of industry have overtaken the aptly named village of Sturton-Le-Steeple, Nottinghamshire, which succumbed to the building of a power station some ten years ago. Literally in this man's back garden, the station has provided work for many like him who were pleased to leave the land for better paid, if less absorbing labour

Once an indispensable part of the
country estate, this lodge, with its
individual architecture was probably the
home of the gamekeeper. Today such
lodges are likely to be leased to old
family retainers

# The Church and the Pub

The church has business at the hatching, matching and dispatching of people they say, and the Bible has a word or two about man taking a little wine for his stomach's sake. A great many villages grew around the church and the alehouse at which the traveller stopped for the night and it was perhaps because of the necessity for both spiritual and bodily comfort that the two were never in real contention. The pious might deplore the impiety of those who looked too long upon the wine and authority sometimes intervened when the inn harboured too many disreputable characters, but over the centuries both institutions flourished because both filled an important need. There is hardly a village of any size that doesn't have a church, generally the established church and sometimes a chapel for good measure and few indeed without a pub, and sometimes more than one. The church is often very old because there was a day for church building. The chapels date from a decade or two of ardent evangelism or dissent.

A cynic might suggest that church, chapel and pub ultimately achieve the same purpose — a content induced by hypnosis or alcohol, and a tempering of the harsh reality of daily life. If the harvest fails the countryman needs to be able to accept the blow. If he loses his job the labourer has a day-to-day misery that can be banished by a tankard of beer or a glass of scrumpy when he can find the money to pay for it. The pub has a free and easy atmosphere in which he can talk out his troubles. The church once had the confessional, but if it has unwisely abandoned this solace, the villager enjoys a touch of ritual and the sound of music.

Singing hymns and listening to the sermon involve a certain concentration and self-discipline and the vicar is well aware of the needs of his congregation. They expect comfort and he offers them comfort even if he can do very little about ruined barley, the failure of the sugar beet, or the slump in the price for lamb or beef. He deals mainly with spiritual matters but he also passes on items of news when the parochial council has at last decided to do something about the leaking roof, the asthmatic organ or the heating system. He reminds his congregation of the milestones in the calendar, the vicarage tea party, the flower show, the harvest festival and the passion play. He reminds the bellringers of the weekday practice. Going to worship the village hurries, coming out of church it dallies and blocks the lych gate and the street beyond. People exchange greetings it would have been unseemly to exchange before church. Non-attenders down the street take note of who was there and who was missing, for this too, is an important part of village life. A belief in God, while not universal even among country folk, brings everyone to the church at least three times in their lives, and those who don't attend will tell the vicar that they believe. Vehement dissenters are always regarded as eccentric and there aren't many of them.

The pub, however, covers ground the church couldn't cultivate. Where the church fills a spiritual need the pub supplies a kind of social service. A great amount of business is settled in the pub. The villager who likes a flutter on a horse knows there is a sweep on the Derby or the National down at 'The Wagoner' or 'The Roebuck'. The man who has something to sell offers it in the bar, gets rid of his dog, his backyard fowls, his unwanted bicycle or his worn-out car. The landlord helps the business along, listens and learns and tactfully forgets or, mindful of his licence, informs the local policeman who passes the information on to the collator in the town. Back-scratching of one sort or another is the very essence of life in a rural community and everyone sooner or later learns what everyone else is doing. In the pub too, outings are arranged, though these are more often stag affairs, men-only expeditions to other places where the brew has to be sampled, the opposition beaten at their own game — darts, skittles, dominoes. The landlord often pressgangs his family into service and goes junket-ing himself. A sound relationship with his patrons is vital to his living and he does his best never to offend or seem aloof. The rival pub at the other end of the village will welcome deserters, and over the years faces come and go. The pub is really owned by its patrons. The landlord must know who sits where. A man's seat may be as important as the family pew once was in the church. If the oldest patron dies, everyone knows the line of succession for the cushioned seat by the fire or the winged settle below the window.

Change transforms the pub, though it may make no structural impression on the church except to bring about a more up-to-date form of heating and lighting. A time was when the brewery brought wooden barrels to the yard and the beer was a local brew. The landlord may recall a day when he used to bring jugged beer up from the cellar to serve it at the bar, and every pint he drew was from the wood, but now all is different with fancy pumps, mirror-backed shelves and spirit dispensers, expensive little bags of nuts, onion-flavoured crisps and Panatella cigars to be smoked when someone wins the sweep. The wooden barrels no longer roll like thunder down into the dank cellar but instead there is a clanging of silvery drums of gassed-up beer. In the bar the rickety table has been whisked away to feed woodworm in the back shed and formica and chromed tube have taken its place. No one who is living well and keeping his end up asks for mild; he calls for Danish lager, vodka and lime, snowballs, or rum and coke.

The old men who have lived through many changes sit playing their dominoes in conspiratorial undertones, their voices sometimes completely drowned by the juke box, which is itself interrupted in mid-phrase by the machine-gun rattle of the one-armed bandit. They have them in most villages down this way, the old men will say. The things are greedy for 5p pieces and don't cough up much! Once in a while comes an invasion of 'with it' people from the town and the place is surrounded by cars. The ring of the till frays the nerves of the old men sitting near it. The landlord works under pressure and shouts more than usual. His wife is out of sight making round after round of ham or beef sandwiches. A temporary help, awkward and shy, takes orders for chicken in the basket and scampi and chips. The chicken served its apprenticeship in the battery. The scampi never swam in the Mediterranean or even looked remotely like a scaled-down lobster or a giant prawn. The village deplores the disturbance of the peace, the shouting and the laughter after hours, the cars roaring off up the street and the vandalism that marks and mars the spot where it all took place.

There are as many sorts of village pubs as there are villages, of course. Here and there is a Rip Van Winkle place where the hall is tiled and the grandfather clock ticks loudly, though time seems to have stood still. The place survives somehow with half a dozen regulars who sit an age over every pint. The atmosphere might belong to another century. At any moment a stage coach should pull in with a demand for capons and stilton, brandy or hot-pokered stout. The place really waits to be discovered by the youngsters with the rally car. The landlord hopes they will never come, and the brewery's district manager tells him that only when they do come can he have his alterations, his new sign and the urinal moved from the gable wall! The reek of the urinal doesn't really bother the small number of villagers and farm workers who patronize the place. They are used to old Joe coming in from his pig farm after clearing his slurry ducts. At closing time they all move into the back room with its boarded window. The till is left open and never rings. If the policeman has bidden them goodnight they know he won't be back. When he comes on his once-a-month visit with the inspector the telephone rings beforehand to say that he is on his way.

The change in the church is dependent upon the incumbent and his bishop. When the squire could nominate the parson he could also lean on his employees to make sure they supported his man. The church had the tithe and all was right with the world. Now the rectory is an ivied ruin or gone from the face of the earth. The present-day rates alone would have beggared a rich man. The young vicar tries to run the church for the younger generation. To hold them he must show them that he, too, is with it. Once in a while he outrages the older generation by letting the youngsters have the church hall for an evening. They have been well-tutored in the essentials of a rave-up by the medium of television or through an occasional visit to the bright lights in town. Success on these occasions is measured in decibels of sound and the quality of equipment producing the psychedelic effect. The villagers know what is happening. The dogs bark and the sound drifts far across the adjoining countryside. The policeman intervenes from time to time. The 'jam sandwich' patrol car cruises through the village until after midnight. The vicar says prayers in private, knowing that this is the generation he has to win or he will be preaching over grey and bald heads to empty pews beyond. He fights a losing battle because the young generation wants to get away more than it wants to stay, and contrives to do so, both mentally and physically. The church really preaches to the converted. It never did really win all along the line even when church-going could be enforced by law. Every countryman knows how hard it is to make a sheep eat hay before it is starving, that a horse can't be forced to drink water or a pig got into a cart without a bucket being put over its head!

Whatever the problems of the church in spiritual matters, the landlord of the pub can be sure that as long as he stocks the right thing he will fill his bar. The breweries have a better assessment of man's appetite — his thirst and his need for relaxation.

Gentlemen of the cloth are called on to perform many and diverse duties as well as their ecclesiastical offices, much of their time being spent in simply listening. Here the vicar, whilst attending the May-Day celebrations, lends an ear to a parishioner's problems

Off to church, Kingsland, Herefordshire

Another way to spend Sunday morning

Despite today's juke boxes and
one-armed bandits, there's still nothing
to beat making one's own entertainment

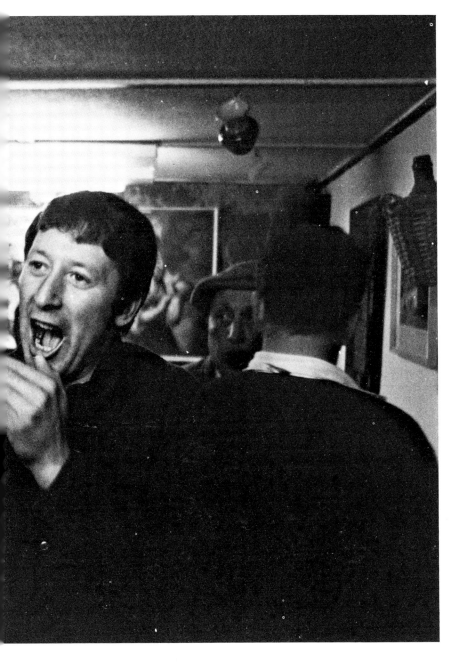

Like part of the furniture, a regular in
his corner of the snug

# Some Members of the Community

Undoubtedly the structure of society in rural areas has derived from a certain autocracy inherited from times when the power of the landowner was absolute. The squire, in his day, relied upon the rector and the schoolmaster to implement his will. The world comprised those who had means, however modest, and those who were poor. No one was greatly concerned about class. A gentleman was a gentleman and a servant knew his place. The squire's place was ultimately taken by people with sufficient means to buy him up piecemeal. A degree of autonomy developed where there had been little or none before. A more radical approach to parochial affairs has come to depend, not so much on the rector and the schoolmaster as minions of authority higher up the scale, as upon a professional class, the retired admiral, the army man, the solicitor or the successful businessman retired to the country. People with a talent for organization and an interest in the welfare of the community find common ground and provide leadership in the face of restrictions government tends to impose without consultation. Village Hampdens are far from commonplace and tyrants are generally more easily routed by retired soldiers and lawyers ! The village accepts the self-interest of its champions more readily than it accepted the patronage of the squire and his churchman, for it is almost impossible to be without it. Leaders of the rural community are familiar figures. The parish knows all there is to know about them, good and bad, and trusts them accordingly.

A community of any sort exists and survives only when it is part of a society in which there are people supplying its immediate needs and performing those services by which the community itself is integrated. In the country the trades, professions and services followed or provided by members of the village or rural population are diverse and wide-ranging. The community needs a man who can put up fences, clear a drain or ditch, catch its moles, and kill its rats, drive the roadroller, the milk lorry or the post office van. It also needs a variety of people who make-and-mend, jacks-of-all-trades who can put a slate on a roof, tiles on a barn, build a stone wall, attend to plumbing or plastering or service a car. The village grocer may combine his business with that of postmaster. If someone needs a light in the back kitchen there is sure to be someone who can do it, just as there is a man who can lay a drain or build a cupboard. The painter can put down a bit of asphalt, for there is no demarcation in the country and a great need for a man to have a stab at the thing.

Everything is expected of the village shop. It needs to be open from morning to night. If a cottager breaks the teacups she needs to replace them without contemplating the loss of a day travelling in to town on the one bus that runs sometimes no more than two or three days in a week. The shop must also provide a great variety of things from a packet of tea to a pair of tights. When people are forced to go into town they buy enough to make the time and the fare worth the journey so that a lot of unsold stock may accumulate on the shelf of the village shop as a result. Television tells the villager what she might expect in town. The village shop must do its best to keep up with demand. It is no use telling a villager there is no call for the thing. She is not to be fobbed off with that kind of excuse.

The post office may be a hole-in-the-corner of the small shop but here everything becomes official. Here the old people come to draw their pensions and everything that requires scrutiny is duly scrutinised by the postmistress who can find the form, explain the official jargon and the rigmarole required by the civil service before it parts with money.

The law, criminal rather than civil, is the concern of the police office. In the front room of the policeman's house are to be seen, full face and profile, the villains who might once in a lifetime pass that way. There is a smell of disinfectant and a couple of correspondence trays beside a heavy typewriter which the policeman manfully pounds with the forefingers of each hand. The law, according to the notices on the constabulary board outside, is really about the Firearms Act, swine fever, foot and mouth and the keeping of wild birds or taking them with birdlime. Only the constable who pins up the notices ever reads them. They discolour in the rain, bleach in the sun and are replaced with amended issues bringing everything up to date, should anyone want to study them.

The policeman does his paperwork and gets his official black bicycle from its shed and rides off on his public relations errand, stopping to talk to people in the village about anything and everything. Once in a while he investigates a complaint and delivers a summons. He gets to know who has had a parking ticket in town and who had to spend a night in the cells there after supping too much beer. He doesn't hound the locals for their minor transgressions. They acknowledge his authority when he is forced to exert it. They call him by his first name and he is on the same terms of familiarity with them. He plays bowls and darts in their company. Discretion makes him share his custom between the two pubs rather than sup the brew he prefers. He finds it impossible to turn out for the cricket team as a regular. Unlike the policeman on the town beat, he is expected to be on duty all round the clock. It wouldn't do if he had to leave the wicket at a run to answer an urgent summons from his divisional command.

When his beat is a long one the authority gives him a little van and he tours the countryside, showing his face where he knows it will be marked, and keeping his eye on the car left too long in a layby or tucked into the old quarry. He learns a lot from the man driving the tractor on the other side of the hedge and the gamekeeper who is on the lookout for poachers using a rifle. In return for his co-operation with the estate he gets invited to the cock shoot in January, when the estate has really had its days at pheasants, and only the cock birds are being shot. The farmers too, take care to keep on the right side of the law and know they can call on the village policeman for help in

things not exactly listed under 'useful police powers' or 'arrestable offences'.

The grapevine operates with little short of the speed of light it sometimes seems because everyone is interested in what everyone else is up to. Gossip is an essential part of everyday life in the country. People would wilt without the stimulation of titbits of news and idle information growing in significance and volume as they are passed on. A shepherd learns that his old van has been repaired but will never pass the MOT, before the garage has sent him word to the effect. A woman five miles out from the village hears that the grocer has just put a basket of plums on his doorstep and they are fifteen pence a pound. The information comes with the mail van or the creamery lorry on tour to drop off empty churns and collect full ones.

Another part of this great rural network depends on the visit of the district nurse, the doctor and the vet. As result of these contacts the countryside will hear that a farmer has become a grandfather, his favourite mare has foaled, or he has had to have a prize cow put down. The vet in particular is at the beck and call of the rural community for it is out there that the really important things happen. He must go when called. He struggles with a frightened beast on the soiled straw of an outhouse and performs emergency surgery on the spot. He delivers a foal or a calf, cleans himself up and goes off back into the black night wondering where he will have to go in the morning. In his hands may lie the future of a good herd of Friesians or Ayrshires, or the life of a show-jumper with a great reputation. He hurries from the herd to the shepherd lambing among straw bales and soon has his needles out and the hypodermic charged with serum. They expect miracles from him and he sometimes performs them. Often they knew his father who had the practice before him. He is more important in the scheme of things than his doctor counterpart.

The doctor competes with superstition, if not witchcraft, and he knows it. They send for him late rather than early when the kind of thing they always did before doesn't seem to be working. He knows their occupational ailments, rheumatism and arthritis, farmer's lung and occasionally the horrors of such things as cattle ringworm in humans — once in a lifetime, something like anthrax. He treats their strains and pains, wins one, and loses one when an overextended farmer is brought down like a tree by a coronary which the intensive care unit at the county hospital can't beat. He looks in on the oldest inhabitant of the village and wonders what longevity is all about when the oldest inhabitant could have died a half dozen times over, yet sits there looking out at the street and sometimes is put out to get the sun like a greatly cherished potplant.

The oldest inhabitant never dies for there is always an instant successor. The carpenter gets each one in turn and runs him up a coffin from a store of coffin sets. The grave-digger comes into his own and the church and the vicar have urgent mid-week business, to which the organist and even the choir may be summoned on occasions.

Marriage is a Saturday event for the most part with a show for those who love dressing-up affairs and the horseplay that goes with the business of 'getting wed'. The organist excels himself with voluntaries, well-known hymns and a bit of Handel for good measure. The bride and groom go off as fast as their hire will carry them — once they have kindled the reception. The revels go on until the guests have had enough and sometimes more than enough, foregetting the names of the bride and groom as well as the way home!

It takes all sorts to make this country community, providing it with pop and peanuts, tangerines and wrapped bread. It takes all sorts to clear a blocked drain, clean a chimney with a gorse bush, a rope and a stone, clear rats from an infested henrun and get rid of the wasps that beleaguer the old two-holed privvy. A little money changes hands for some of these essential services but some of them are more easily obtained in return for a few eggs, a bag of apples, some string beans or freshly-dug potatoes. Payment in kind is one of the traditional ways of making the wheels go round in the country and everyone is ready for a deal and a bargain. In the market they spit on money for luck, clap a hand to seal the agreement, or spend hours haggling, walking away, complaining and having second thoughts about almost everything man may buy or offer for sale, from a couple of laying hens to a pony, a goat in milk to a load of firewood. Commerce with or without the passing of silver is in the country's lifeblood. The object of labour in the field or the garden is to earn a man's bread and whatever the man does may be translated if not in to pounds and pence, in to potatoes and eggs, butter and cottage cheese, nets of carrots or even bales of hay.

The ramifications of it all are endless and impossible to follow as people go about their business. The taxman, who is surely the most unloved official anywhere, would never be able to correctly assess the final benefit and tax the profit accrued. He knows this. The countryman doesn't profess to be clever. It pays him not to be thought so. How can a man who left school at fourteen and never got beyond 'the three Rs' be smart enough to fool the Inland Revenue? The simple fellow protests that he is ignorant. He blames no one. Everyone can't be clever, can they? That should be answer enough. It generally has to be when a couple of bales of hay change hands to purchase a Christmas turkey and a butchered lamb pays for a bit of rewiring in the outhouses. The rural community has always operated on this basis. Once again, it is a way of life and a person has to belong to understand or even get the feel of it.

Everything is expected of the village shop. The indispensable shopkeeper and some of her customers outside Redwick village stores, Gwent

The country policeman who still has a
more leisurely life than his city
counterpart

The undisputed grapevine, this farmer has an eggs and cream round in a small Devon village

The country vet attending to one of a Friesian herd in the course of his rounds

44

On a blazing hot day this Radnorshire
man takes his ease while his flock run
on

A soldier's wedding, Swainswick Parish Church

This old woman, like many cottagers, keeps a few hens for company, for their eggs and occasionally for use as table birds. In days gone by she might have been taken for a witch. Today she merely tells fortunes at local fairs

Explaining to her customers the various uses of her plants, this herb and flower seller plies her trade at Abergavenny Market

# The Fabric of Rural Life

What the women of the present century inherited from their nineteenth century counterparts was good housekeeping and a standard that required the best to be made of everything to hand. The creativity of women and their single-mindedness in pursuit of any objective puts their male counterparts to shame. The rural community of women was rich in talent, full of know-how and eager to share their culinary and domestic secrets. The Women's Institute, while it was formed for the improvement of the quality of life in rural communities, to a degree, simply co-ordinated what was there and channelled the ability of its recruits into something that has been a wonderful outlet for many thousands of countrywomen. Its branches were restricted to communities of 4,000 or less. This meant that it gathered in the women of the rural areas and the village. Its influence for the good of the community could hardly be measured in terms of therapy by the development of crafts and arts.

The Institute has flourished with the aid of only a little professional instruction. Its strength comes from its membership and in every rural community there are women whose leisure and interest in life would undoubtedly be restricted without it. Who wants to bottle fruit, make a dress, pickle walnuts, embroider a sampler or make a pair of gloves ? Who needs a recipe for a cherry cake, a honey bun or nettle soup ? There is a natural pride in good housekeeping and a rivalry among women in these matters. The village may sometimes rock a little with the repercussions of a confrontation between rivals but the Institute survives and the educational uplift is continual. Members of the Rural Institute who might never have looked for more than a trip to the nearest county town organize a visit to the tulip fields of Holland — and fly there. Their grandmothers probably turn in their graves at the thought of the dangers of such an expedition. They would need sal volatile to recover from the news that these simple country women flew by jet clutching in their hands on the way back not smelling salts but souvenir bottles of Bols ! Could such women ever sit darning socks again, or content themselves putting up bottles of chutney or jars of preserve ?

The wonderful thing about the Institute is that it achieves exactly what it was set up to achieve, the improvement of life in the rural community, not only for the women who find an outlet for their many and varied talents, but for their menfolk and their families as well. Why shouldn't a villager fly to Holland, or to the other end of the earth for that matter, and return stimulated with all she has seen, the fields and villages of France or the rural settlements of Scandinavia ?

The need for social contact between women is recognized if not always by their menfolk, at least by the church, people concerned with health and social welfare and those intelligent women who love to organize things. It is from the more casual contact of church membership that a great many other recreational outlets are cultivated. The vicar encourages the ladies who would like to decorate the church on special occasions, the born flower arrangers. He gently talks one or two into joining the sewing guild. Some country women are very shy and lacking in self-confidence. Some love to belong and would help, even if they could contribute little more than an ability to lay out a table of cups and saucers for the inevitable tea-drinking and biscuit-nibbling these meetings always include. The bring-and-buy and the jumble sale becomes very like taking in one another's washing and the sharp-eyed villager recognizes non-consumable offerings that have passed from cottage to cottage over the course of years.

There are a great many avenues of activity to be explored in raising funds for the repair of the church, providing a party for the old people, a Christmas revel for the youngsters. The business is hardly ever at an end in a lively community. Committees sit and sub-committees may result. People who are outside the organization are co-opted on or made honorary members. The influence of the vicar is felt here and there. He is consulted at times. He is careful not to make his influence a dominating factor in what the women do, for he knows that once they take sides he may find himself in a hornet's nest. His place is really in the wings or in the background. He leaves things to the women and the women come to him for his final approval.

Sometimes the activity of the female population is diverted from culinary art, sewing and handicraft, to the putting on of a pageant of one sort or another. The country-dweller, male or female, loves spectacle, pageantry and mime. Like the secrets of housewifery and the recipes they have inherited, pageants and the crowning of village queens has been handed down to them from the distant past. Weeks and sometimes months of preparation go into these events. The sewing women sew, the dress-makers work frantically cutting out dresses from patterns. The coal lorry will be borrowed, a dozen reluctant boys conscripted to squire the small girls of the queen's retinue of hand-maidens. The whole thing will carry a growing excitement that will fray tempers and make youngsters leave their supper uneaten. The menfolk will be drawn in to help decorate the street and marshal the parade. There will be canned music and perhaps an amplifier to assist the chief marshal in making his voice heard. The sound of music will carry a couple of miles. A newly-made queen or princess of the next village will be there with her attendants and the subjects of both queens will compare notes. When all is over there will be streamers draped on the bushes, paper roses lying along the street, and here and there a truck or a van left with the coloured crepe still hung about it. The sun has shone or it has rained. It was a great day. The dresses were never so pretty but Old Mrs So-and-so was never in bed until one o'clock, so much sewing did she have to do!

There are other local institutions in various places that have stemmed from the mummers and Morris dancers of long ago, events that involve the observation of rites, the origin of which even the organizers can't explain – dressing up in top hats, begging from the spectators, playing instruments and dancing. Rituals have been created and developed to awe, or amuse and delight audiences over a long period of time. Who cares what it really means so long as it continues to be done every year, like the beating of the bounds? The people involved in these special rites dance and dress up, put old battered tall hats or even formidable sets of horns on their heads, instructed by old performers who remember the way they were taught the ritual. The village and people who have come in to watch take it all as gospel. What was always done must always be done. A pageant is a pageant and a dance must have movements. The performers are less self-conscious than the village queen and her retinue, but that is to be expected. No one makes fun or thinks the thing outlandish. It is part of the life of the old village. It came down from the people of the first Queen Elizabeth's time, when everyone wore gaiters and smocks and the music of the mandolin and the fiddle kept the feet of the dancers clattering on the flags.

The fair and the feast, with which the mime and dance were once integrated, have gone. There were too many fairs and too many feasts in the old days it seems. The law restricted them because too many cadgers and beggars, pickpockets and horse-thieves would congregate in these places. The Puritans forbade them, considering the Morris dance an ungodly performance, although it couldn't be suppressed everywhere so long as there was music and someone who knew the dress and the steps of the dance. Give the villager the smallest excuse and he will revive a thing because he has respect for the old customs, even when he converts a stable into a garage and applies for permission to knock down a building of historic interest.

There are of course, other village institutions and events that are not in any way historical or deriving from ancient custom. The flower show, for instance, the vicarage party where some play croquet on the lawn and others dip in the bran tub, guess the weight of the cake, or the number of beans in a bottle. The show attracts the best from the village gardens in the way of flowers and vegetables. Villagers are great gardeners and know how to grow good vegetables. The flowers were the pride of every cottager until the show came up and then they were harvested for the judges, who come from over the hill, and are expected to be impartial in their assessment of a display of roses, a bunch of long carrots or a vegetable marrow. The women of the Institute vie with one another in offerings of rock buns, melting moments and biscuits. There will be pots of raspberry jam and jars of honey and lemon curd.

Later on another sort of show may occupy the hall, for besides having a flair for flowers and vegetables, country people are fond of breeding almost every sort of bird and animal from bantams to Belgian hares. The children of the place will struggle to bring their rabbits and the highly-groomed family cat or dog. Their fathers will supply some of the fur and feather that gives the society its name. The

A quiet rural pastime; watching the life in the village street

Carnival Day; the womenfolk of the village display a lively imagination in this Miss . . . fancy dress competition

The carnival Queen's attendants awaiting her arrival

judges may not be equally expert on white mice and Old English rabbits with butterfly noses, but they will do their best. No one pretends that the show is anything like a national event. It is an outlet for the competitive spirit. Every entrant knows his rabbit or pet bird is better than the one that took the prize, and the prize, in any case, was only a packet of birdseed or bran for the guineapig.

Where the community thrives its institutions are strong. Where it declines, its institutions diminish and their diminishing is a symptom of ultimate death more often than not. Basically, however, where the reason for the village being where it is remains, its life is healthy and where people are happy they create a product of their happiness – the Institute, the institution, the flower show, the fur and feather show, the Morris dancers' group, the sewing guild, the young mothers' group and the sisterhood. The small community is one in which everyone is directly involved with everyone else. The fabric of rural life may be an open weave, but its fibres are strong and at this moment, despite the depopulation of the countryside, the yarn, the fibre of that fabric, remains strong.

More important than the sheepdog
trials, a discussion between two elderly
gentlemen

A Boy's Brigade on their way to church
service at Tintern in the Wye Valley

A Silver Band at the local agricultural
show. Oblivious to his audience, this
small boy acts out his role as conductor

Sometimes the excitement is too much when you're not very old, and any bit of shade is welcome on a hot day

The fairground has its own mystery and even if this old merry-go-round, still worked by hand and possibly the last of its kind in the country, does not give thrills and spills to the children of Ludlow, Shropshire, it conjures up nostalgic memories for the older inhabitants. The hand-carved, painted gallopers are now becoming collector's items

The travelling circus and menagerie were here. Now at the end of it all, a little girl bids goodbye to the nanny goat's kid

The real English country garden with vegetables on one side and flowers on the other

# Sports and Pastimes

Like his town counterpart, the man who lives in the country would rather be a participant in the sport he follows than a mere spectator. The vicariousness of viewing, even from a grandstand, is never as exhilarating as taking part. Alas for the countryman who isn't a landowner or a man of considerable means, the three field sports he would take up are expensive. He has no choice but to be a spectator at the meet. He may be a beater at the shoot. He can watch the salmon going smoothly up from one pool to another but he can rarely hope to fish the best beats where salmon are easily taken.

To be a member of a hunt calls for a supporting subscription, the upkeep of a horse or the money to hire one, and the accoutrements that go with it. What the watching countryman enjoys is the spectacle. He sees very little of the chase for the fox is disobliging and is never put up on the green or outside the old inn where the meet assembles. When everyone is present, and at the appointed time, the pack moves off, with the master cantering beside his professional huntsman. The whips crack and hounds are rebuked for their high spirits or a tendency to dally by the way. Then the cavalcade passes and the spectators hurry to climb on rails or walls to see the pack draw the first stand of gorse and bracken, or quickly work their way through the unfenced copse and down to the wood beyond. There, for the people who have come to see what is to be seen, the business ends. One or two may have cars and trundle off to some vantage point, where, if they are lucky, they may see hounds at full stretch and the field strung out behind them. Once in a long time they may catch a glimpse of the fox. More often than not the fox is as elusive as a cock pheasant in the rushes of the marsh. The hounds yelp once or twice away out there on the rolling fields, the horn sounds faintly, but all that remains is a swinging gate someone forgot to close and the churned-up mud where the field suddenly put their heels to the flanks of their mounts because someone cried that the fox was off down the side of a hedge.

There are many versions of what fox hunting is about. It is certainly not about the rationality of a man doing his best in the most practical way to get rid of a predator. The killing of a fox is a by-product. It is not really an excuse for dressing up, though some fashionable hunts may occasionally seem to be more concerned with socializing than hunting – until the dedicated few prove that clothes do not make the man who would be there at the end of the day! Hunting is really about the chase. Stripped of all the emotive words that are applied to the business by supporters or detractors, there remains only a primitive love of hunting an animal through cover and across the open plain, on foot or on horseback, with a pack of specially bred hounds. This satisfies a very strong human instinct. Unfortunately not everyone can afford to gratify his urges and indulge natural instinct. Fox-hunting thrives not on the goodwill of the countryman half as much as on the money of hunt subscribers. It isn't put on as a spectacle for the entertainment of the rural population. It isn't even arranged at the convenience of the farming community. It takes place because it is exciting, it has a ritual, and it requires a certain stamina and endurance to stay with the people up front through mud and thorns, over walls and across formidable deep streams and crumbling-banked ditches. The outcry against it has little effect upon the numbers who subscribe to the many hunts to be found all over Britain. The words blood sports are highly emotive, but the hunting man, and many countrymen, will say quite simply that fishing, shooting and hunting are a way of life their critics really know little about. The occasional misguided defence – in the case of fox-hunting – that the use of a pack of twenty couple of hounds with twice as many men and horses is the only humane and reasonable way to control the fox – simply plays into the hands of critics. Fox-hunting never was about either the keeping down of foxes or their extermination. On the contrary, good hunting country is one in which the fox is encouraged even when the gamekeeper may suffer losses on his rearing field.

Shooting driven game, either on the moor or on arable land, is another field sport largely the prerogative of the wealthy. The cultivation of game is a business not unlike the rearing of livestock on the farm. The pheasant isn't there as a wild species in any number that would permit it to be driven over guns and the 'sporting gentleman' tends to be sedentary. He prefers to wait at a stand over which the keeper contrives to have the birds driven. To this end the keeper begins to catch up pheasants in the first months of the year, using the eggs he gets from them to hatch chicks in a thermostatically-controlled incubator and a highly efficient brooder. After this, by his diligent attention, he will have a great many young poults to rear and feed and finally establish in his covers. After protecting these rather tame young pheasants for several months, driving them in and feeding them day after day, he will finally, with the help of his beaters, drive them out again to be shot down. The cost per bird will be many times what the game-dealer who buys the bag will be able to pay for them, or charge his customer. It is not the habit of the sporting gentleman to have his sport costed out for him. He prefers not to know and he hardly ever discusses the economics of the thing, though he is pleased to say that he provides some employment for the keeper and his helpers.

There is, of course, another side to the field sport of shooting. A great many countrymen were brought up to the gun and are what are sometimes scornfully called pot-hunters. They take a dog and a gun and find the wild pheasant, the partridge covey on the farm outside the shooting estate, the mallard along the stream and the hare that haunts the field of winter wheat. With a great deal more enthusiasm than the stockbroker who sets himself firmly on his shooting stick with his hammerless ejectors loaded by a man at his elbow, the rough shooter takes his sport where he finds it and makes a modest bag of

a brace of pheasants once in a while. When he can't afford to rent a few acres of rough shooting the modest countryman will often join a wood pigeon or wildfowling club and shoot pigeons on the corn field or mallard on the marsh. Pigeons do a great amount of damage to crops. Even the mallard can do as much harm to a barley field as a high wind that breaks the straw and leaves the heads where the combine can't harvest them.

The sport of fishing is widespread and if the best salmon rivers and the best trout streams are, like the fashionable hunt and the best shooting, always in the hands of those with the most money, the less affluent countryman may have his fishing by virtue of ownership of a small stretch of bank, membership of a fishing club, or the occasional ticket on the hotel water, taken when the river is just right. The visitor is at a disadvantage because he must stay in a local hotel and wait for things to come right, or have a fast car and a motorway close at hand so that he can come rushing down when things are in his favour and fish are running.

Beyond this branch of fishing there is the ever-popular sport of coarse fishing. Here the local is only elbowed out by the powerful fishing club with a large membership recruited in industrial areas. He may nevertheless know a pond or a lake in which there are good carp or big pike. He has access to secret places where he can take a good tench, catch fine roach or rudd, perch or chub, parking himself, like the townee angler, once in a while under a large umbrella to sit there watching his float and the flight of the dragon fly. He has done this kind of thing since boyhood and knows as much about the habits and habitat of the fish he catches as most experts will ever know. If there is a good place he learned about it from his father or his grandfather. He caught the big trout in the mill sluice before the millwheel was paralysed by rust and the erosion of the gear it turned. He knows all about the big pike in the drain. There was always one there and it was always taken on a small rudd or a minnow. It hangs in a glass cask in the hall of the local hotel, its green flanks getting darker and its white flecks dulling a little every year. The glass case has cracked. All the locals remember when that pike was caught. The marvellous thing is that it is still there in the drain waiting to be caught once again.

Apart from field sports, which include such things as rook shoots and hare drives, the countryman has a number of pastimes that are traditional – village cricket, for instance, with the essential element of partisanship and a much more exciting, 'have-a-go' game than that blessed by the MCC. Summer wouldn't be summer without the cross-country sound of a bat hitting a ball followed by the hilarious shouts of that mixed gallery of old men and enthusiastic boys. The local game goes back to the maypole and a time when a cricket side had to carry the good name of the place wherever it played – and set out early because there was no car or bus to whirl them from place to place. Everyone who lives in the village wants to know how the side

got on against their greatest rivals. For some reason, football rarely produces the same enthusiasm. The old men watch cricket. The younger men play and, with the passing of time, graduate to the bowling green where they compete one against the other as they do at darts, skittles and dominoes in the pub. Here and there those with a love of singing join a choir or a glee club, take up choral singing and compete against societies in other districts. Dancers dance — old time dances, traditional country dances. Gardeners join the gardening club and pigeon-fanciers breed homing pigeons and send them off on training flights before entering them in competition. The rural community naturally groups itself into clubs and societies of different sorts. People travel a long way for their enjoyment and the social contact these activites bring. Where the need is greatest the enthusiasm is always strongest. There is no busier joiner than the countryman who finds his isolation rather too much to bear.

The huntsman doffs his cap to subscribers as the pack moves off

Bringing up the rear two members of the hunt move quietly forward, listening for the sound of the horn

Drawing the first cover, the huntsman,
followed by the whipper-in, leads his
pack down a woodland track

Village boys may not be able to afford the expensive sport of shooting driven game but an early morning duck flight gives them an equal chance of testing their skill

Foot-followers with a basset hound

Fishing is this country's greatest participant sport. Every weekend large numbers of coarse fishermen from town and country come to compete in match events or sit in contemplation by the water

Game fishing is a different art, requiring
not only the skill and patience to cast
again and again, but the means to be
able to afford a day's fishing on an
expensive river

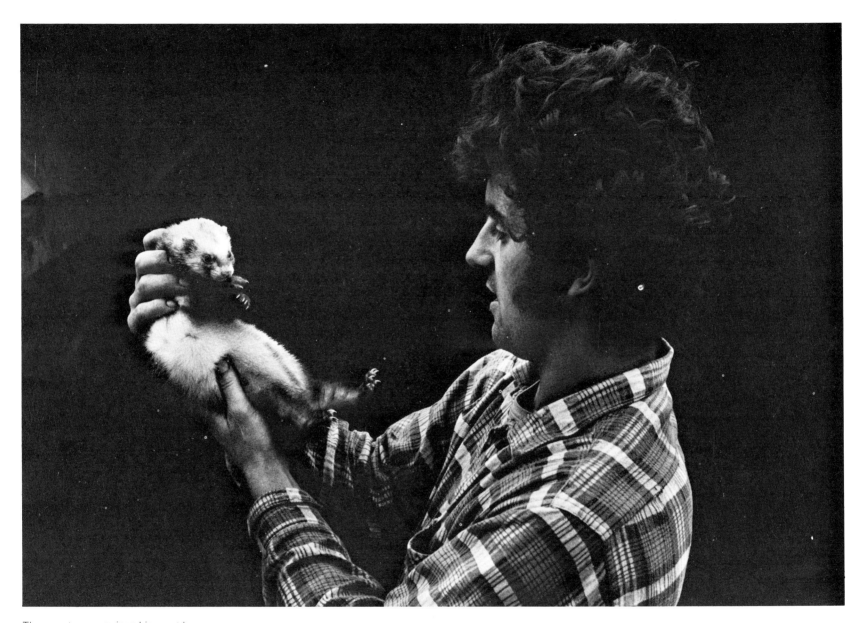

The countryman enjoys his sport in
many less expensive ways than shooting
game and the ferret provides both a
day's excitement and a brace of rabbits
for the pot

You have to be up early and full of
enthusiasm to pick a basket of
mushrooms

Soaked to the skin and trailing their net behind them, would-be poachers leave the river without their expected fish

# Trade and Craft

In the continual change that takes place in every sphere of life, old ways of doing things become too slow or entirely obsolete, so that those who follow trades or crafts, and have provided services no longer required, become almost entirely redundant. There was a time when there was a flour mill within what was a day's travel for a horse and cart, and a blacksmith and wheelwright to be found within the same radius. The miller has gone and the mill is obsolete. The wheelwright is hard to find inside a whole county, so infrequently are his services needed, and the horses no longer queue for their turn at the smithy. Instead the smith goes out to shoe them.

A sentimentalist might prefer to ignore the fact that while a thatched roof can be a very snug insulation from the cold of winter and the extreme heat of summer perhaps, it is also far less durable than slate. When it lets in water or is penetrated by birds or mice, as frequently happens, there is a serious problem to be faced. Thatchers, like wheelwrights, are hard to find. The craft became unfashionable centuries ago, not just because it required the very best wheat straw or reeds but because other roof coverings could be applied with less effort. A slater is a tradesman who, once the joiner has done his work, needs only ladders and a good supply of slates to cover a roof in a day or so. The thatcher's work must be more painstaking to keep everything firm and watertight. The repair of a slate roof may not call for a skilled tradesman, but the repair of thatch certainly does, and the thatcher knows how and where to begin. Thatchers where they are to be found, are generally father and son or brothers working together, with no shortage of work because maintenance is always needed somewhere. There are hundreds of thatched dwellings and old pubs dotted about the countryside even today. The thatcher will be there only so long as there is this work for him to do. When the work so diminishes that the thatcher can't live the trade will die out. There is very little else that a thatcher may turn his skills to.

A wheelwright, by contrast, is an artificer in wood. He can work as well in pine or oak as he can in beech, ash or elm. He can turn his hand to the work a joiner and carpenter has been doing and this in fact, is what has happened. While not every country joiner is able to make a wheel with spokeshave, mallet and chisel, the wheelwright can use joinery tools to make a living. Today the wheelwright is a rare bird. When he is offered work it is much more likely to be for the occasional gig or four-in-hand, governess cart, or dogcart that a collector prizes. The world of the wooden wheel depends upon people who collect things and take a delight in preserving and keeping them in good condition. There is no call for a set of wheels for a haywain or a Scotch cart because the workhorse has gone from the scene. There is no mews from which might trundle a string of hansoms and well-sprung flies. The wooden wheel itself is a collector's item. When it is unearthed from the back of some old shed it is painted and varnished to lean against a wall as a byegone. No one needs to tell the wheelwright he is redundant almost everywhere.

The blacksmith's survival depends on what might once have been called the genteel trade or the carriage business that kept the innkeeper going – people with money to indulge themselves a little by keeping a couple of hunters, show ponies, trekking ponies, little fat cobs or discreet hacks. The pony was never as popular – or as expensive – as it is today. A great many country people keep ponies or have an interest in pony events at the local show. The smith who once toiled almost day and night to put shoes on plough teams and horses to be pressed into service for harvest, finds himself on call to service these pleasure riders. At the forge the pony will be hot shod, the shoes fitted hot from the fire and bedded on the nail of the foot as they cool. This is the perfect way of shoeing a horse. A shoe is generally held by seven nails – a heavy horseshoe may have eight nails, but seven is the ideal number – and, apart from the cleat at the front, the nails are all that keep it on the animal's foot when it exerts itself to trot or canter on hard ground. A well-bedded shoe will come loose less easily and, as the general preparation for cold shoeing is of necessity less effective, no matter how thoroughly it is done, cold shoes have a less long life. Unfortunately for the smith, popular though the riding pony has become, he finds that people are reluctant to come to him. A horse located at some distance away may have a shoe missing or might be in danger of being lamed on the long ride to the smithy. It isn't every horse owner who has a horsebox and a car he can use to take the pony to the forge. The smith must go to the horse.

When he is in a countryside where pony-breeding and riding are a thriving business the smith can make a good living attending these animals. Where the trade is not so good he must turn his skill to other uses. He made this choice, or had it made for him, years ago when the implement trade began to die on him and the agricultural depot began to stock spares for machinery the tractor pulled. The smith became a welder rather than an artificer in metals. He used acetylene gas and tacked things together instead of forging them on the coal fire. He kept his fire for horseshoes but got rid of the bellows and installed a blower fan, which was just as well since there was no apprentice to work the old bellows or learn the art of fusing iron with a hammer on the anvil. The modern smith makes a set of gates for someone in the village or even supplies them to a builder who keeps them in stock. He welds a car body and does a temporary repair on the implement some impoverished farmer may not be able to afford to throw away. He sometimes produces wrought-iron work that sells to people who have artistic ideas for the improvement of a house they are renovating. This side of the business may provide a creative outlet for a craftsman who loves to do scrolling and design articles with some artistic merit, but the average blacksmith in the country has his living to make. He is concerned with more practical things. The day when the smith made ploughs and other implements used on the farm will never return. The call is for a mechanic servicing things mass produced in industrial areas.

There are other crafts that here and there provide those of particular skill with a modest living. Hurdle-makers and basket-makers, for instance, ply their trades in districts where there is good coppice wood or willow or sallow available for the making of durable baskets of different sorts. The hurdle-maker competes with the factory supplying a similar item in galvanized iron but he sells his product in his own district and his overheads are less. Hurdles are used for penning sheep and calves and sometimes for temporary gates. Both crafts are specialized and are almost certain to be handed down in the family. In a district where there are more conifer woods than deciduous trees the craft may be rustic work, using barked poles or split poles. Here, however, the skill involved in making things is less. The product will never weather as well and will have to be treated with creosote. It generally consists of benches, rustic seats, sheds and summerhouses, the material for which may be bought from the local estate or the Forestry Commission.

Builders in stone, men who have the skill in walling and drystone work, follow yet another trade that has fewer and fewer recruits and has its own particular know-how. The use of stone with or without mortar – in the Lake District wonderful examples of weatherproof unmortared stone work are to be seen everywhere – is more than the mason's art. The waller who undertakes this kind of thing is always on the books of the local builder and the local authority. Today we may not build many houses of stone. A mason-built, stone house would cost more than a millionaire would care to spend and it would be hard to recruit a team of men to cut the stone and build the house. There is, nevertheless, a great call for chimneywork in stone, or low walls to set off a property. Stone walls that are part of many public enclosures have to be repaired, renovated and rebuilt at times.

The craft is practised in slightly different ways in parts of the country where the local stone is different – sandstone here, limestone there, a soft yellow stone in Lincolnshire, a warm stone in the Cotswolds, granite in the north. The nature of the stone always governs the length of time the craftsman is on the job. It doesn't take very long to dress sandstone with modern equipment, but it takes a long time to cut granite. Limestone is often mortared on the outside and rubble-cored to save material and speed up the work. Drystone-walling (there are still occasional competitions in which the wallers of a particular district will take part) is a very different business and again it depends on the nature of the stone in a locality. Where the rock strata allow flat-sided pieces to be used, the building of the wall presents no great problem for a man who knows what he is about. Where he works on land through which the glacier once moved his material will consist largely of rounded boulders. Here he will have to grade his material and turn his boulders as he lays them to make sure that his loose building, with nothing whatsoever to bond the structure, is sound and solid. The waller's work, once again, has been mainly maintenance since the days of the land enclosure acts. The old walls run for mile after mile across the moors. Some of them appear to be there forever. They are, nevertheless, subject to damage by hikers and ramblers, store cattle breaking out or sheep with a wanderlust.

While wallers build walls and thatchers still repair thatch, there are always country joiners or village joineries where all kinds of things needed in the houses round about are made or part-made to be assembled in the farm or cottage. The materials have changed, plywood and blockboard and formica taking the place of old-fashioned red and white deal, pitch pine and oak. The modern joiner puts in a blockboard door or a prefabricated staircase he would once have built in situ. He has gone with the times in his choice of tools too – the electric drill and the sander instead of the old belly brace and the wooden jackplane. His morticing machine is hardly used. He doesn't have a stock of hardwood because not only is oak very expensive, it is old-fashioned in an age when nothing constructed of wood is really what it appears to be on the surface.

One of the most recent crafts to establish itself in the country, or perhaps re-establish itself after a lapse of centuries, is that of the potter. As a rule, today's potter is a product of the art school and sets himself down to make his pots and fire his kiln where pots tend to be entirely plastic or mass-produced things no one really cherishes. It takes time, of course, to imprint the product of the kiln with a local name but a great deal has been done by hopeful potters to achieve this distinction. Many more, like the villagers themselves, depend on the visitor who comes and goes and doesn't really care whether what he sees or enjoys has a special local significance or not. Art is for those who can appreciate it, but money is what it is all about.

The miller; though still in use, his windmill is now more of a tourist attraction than a commercial enterprise

A shortage of thatching material forty years ago resulted in corrugated iron taking the place of thatch on the slopes of roofs facing away from the road. Here at the side of the house the thatcher completes a repair

A sagging, decayed old thatch on a barn contrasts with the snug, firm covering of the newly-thatched farmhouse

The wheelwright; after serving his apprenticeship in 1911, Harold Gogh started his own business and at one time employed coachbuilders and painters. Refusing to retire, he still earns a living by making gig wheels and hayrakes

Farmer making stakes for fences with the aid of a belt-driven saw

Forestry worker

The coalman; turning out in all
weathers, Twin Cribbet on his round in
Princetown, Dartmoor

The blacksmith dresses the hoof after
shoeing a horse

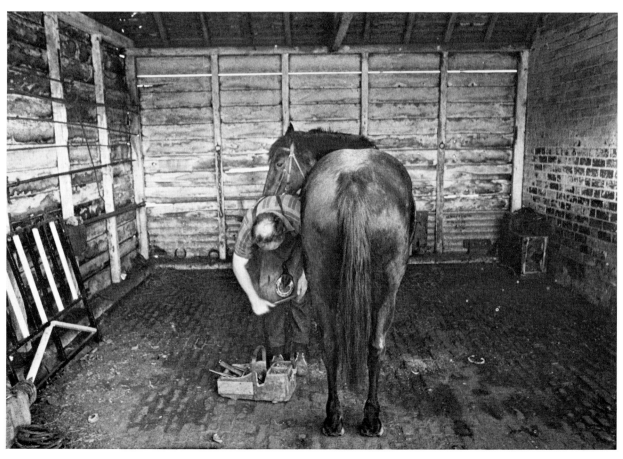

Mr Musgrove, the osier grower, with his harvest ready for basket-making. Westonzoyland, Somerset

Just down the road at Burrowbridge, the basket-maker puts together the finished product

# Life on the Land

Not every countryman works on the land, or would do so given the opportunity. The average countryman knows too much about the hardship of ploughing and sowing and the frustrations of being a farmworker or a farmer, supposing he had the money to be one and had leanings in that direction. The people who live on the land only very infrequently do so from choice. There are easier and certainly more comfortable ways of earning a living. The farmworker is there because his father was there. It seemed the only thing to do when any other sort of work would have required him to leave his family and live away in the town. The farmer is often there because his inheritance was a set of implements, some stock and a tenancy which lingered on into the old age of his parents then finally came to him. Here and there, of course, the farmer inherited the land itself, and land represents labour and care over a long period, an investment any good farmer is reluctant to abandon or sell to an incomer.

There they are, the man whose work prospects diminish year by year — five per cent at the present time — and the man who employs him and worries about his tied cottage, the green pound, the milk cheque and the price of barley. The compensations for living in the country are many but whether they outweigh the benefits of tightening nuts on a car-factory assembly-line or not, only someone who has done both might be able to say. The production line is endless, but the assembly-line worker drops his tools and clocks off, while the farmworker may have the responsibility of lambing ewes who won't line up to have their midwifery done, won't have their lambs within the statutory working week. A cow calves when her time comes. The seed must be sown when the rain has finished. The plough must rip up and down the field if there is to be a crop of winter wheat at the right time of year. The green pound doesn't buy a ticket to a land flowing with milk and honey. Too much milk in one year must be discouraged the next, because partners across the channel have more butter and cheese than they can sell. The farmworker, bumping and bouncing behind the tractor to drag a load of manure to the field, doesn't look like someone involved in economics. Nor does his boss who rattles away in the Land Rover to check the prices at the local market or make a deal for some item of equipment made necessary by the latest turn of events in Brussels.

What does a farmer do when it comes down to it? He cultivates what arable land he has. He raises beef, he tends a flock of sheep — South Downs, Leicesters, black-faces, Herdwicks or some fancy breed in fashion for the quality of its wool. He lives off a herd of Friesians or he keeps battery hens. He does it on a large scale or a small one. He is an expert on sugar beet or lays out a hundred acres of Brussels sprouts beside another hundred of cabbage and cauliflower. He may grow little else but onions or buy in Irish cattle to 'finish' them off. He keeps pigs if he can obtain processed swill and lives far enough from the village for the smell to be dissipated on the summer air.

The farmer's 'man' works with him in any of these branches of the industry. They get on well enough because most of the time they share the labour. Each appreciates the other's problem. They argue about overtime once in a while or about days off that are due. They sometimes call one another by their first names. The worker talks about the boss. Often the worker's father was in the employ of the boss's father and they know all there is to know about one another. The boss lets his man use the van or his Land Rover to go into town at night perhaps, and they have an agreement about certain things a shop steward wouldn't negotiate. They don't often go to market together, for markets are always on working days and the 'man' doesn't go unless he is needed to unload stock or see newly-bought animals safely on the way home.

The tied cottage is a bone of contention only between an unsatisfactory workman and his master, or an unsatisfactory master and his man. It is not a unique institution, when it comes down to it, because all kinds of people already live in the tied cottage or tied house, and drive around in the 'tied' car for that matter. When it goes the worker will perhaps lose a little of the comfortable human relationship he had with a good boss. The good boss may be less inclined to see his man's point of view when he knocks off to drive to the council house several miles away from the scene of operations. The trouble with farming is that it can't be managed within the strict limits of an eight-hour day and clocking-in and clocking-out regulation a factory worker lives with.

The farmworker once went to a hiring fair. Now he applies for the job as advertised in the local paper or *The Farmers Weekly* and what counts, as far as he is concerned, are the perks that go with the job. He may end up, if he has the necessary ability, working on a share basis with his employer. What the farmer wants is the least possible labour turnover and a man he can trust. A good man in charge of his herd is worth his weight in gold and a bad one will ruin him. There was a time when the man with a large family was sure of work where a single man found it difficult to find employment, but the situation has become reversed. There is little need for the family on the land except where they may be required to pick sprouts, strawberries and other soft fruit in season. Even on these occasions casual labour — pickers — are never very hard to find. The casual worker on the land moves with the season, picking peas, lifting onions, ending with the broccoli crop when the potato season is over. On the arable farm even the man who ploughs the field may not be needed at harvest for the contractor may come in to combine the wheat or the barley, leaving him with not even straw to be burned or ploughed in. Between whiles the farmworker who isn't always ploughing or cultivating may be foraging for silage-making, cleaning ditches and drains with special equipment designed for the job, and replacing the old ditcher's long shovel. He may be spraying the field or drilling seed of one sort or another, or cutting the silage he made in spring to feed the standing-in herd in winter. There will be little time to spare for talking about things. Weeds grow while a man stands talking, and if the ground hasn't been sprayed it has to be gone over with the mowing machine.

The recreational outlets for the farmworker are mainly those he creates for himself. He shoots, or occasionally breeds dogs. He keeps a few fowl. When he has some means of transport he takes himself into town for a night out and a Chinese meal. He has little chance to be an active supporter of the football team, and if he has a keen interest in any team game he must be enthusiastic enough to travel rather a long way. He tends to stay at home and 'watch the box', and often his interest in his work takes him back to the job in his spare time, whether his boss asks him to or not. They generally have much the same interests, master and man. The master breeds a pony and rides perhaps, or occasionally he plays golf while his son belongs to the Young Farmers' Club and, if there is enough money, may be a car rally enthusiast. They go to farm sales and the market together. They, and the labourer, will have their day at the county show or the county sports, and meet their own kind at these events. Talk is meat and drink on these occasions and men who haven't met in months will stand rooted to the spot discussing different aspects of farming, the Common Market and all that goes with it, prodding the ground reflectively with their sticks, and remembering things as they used to be.

The world is changing fast in every sphere of farming. Nothing is the same one season to the next. There are hedges to be grubbed out to make combining a more economical proposition, new strains of grass, new dressings to be tried on the seed, new ways of coping with pests and diseases, and remedies for ailments that were once fatal.

The farmworker himself is not the man his father was. He knows the serum to get for mastitis, liver fluke or some other pest that infests cows or sheep, how to artificially inseminate a cow if called upon to do so. He may be a dab hand at stripping an engine, getting an old tractor going, rectifying a fault in some piece of dairy equipment, a pump or a spray. He is a mechanic and not a horse-doctor, which his grandfather may have had to be. He studies the manual and grasps the essentials in servicing. At the agricultural show he hangs round the particular area that deals with his kind of problem — and comes home to try to persuade 'the boss' to go in for something new. The boss has been doing something of the same sort himself. He finally goes along to persuade the bank to lend him money to stay in business, competing with his neighbours who have already managed the improvement. The involvement of the worker with his master is what makes them both secure in their work. An enthusiastic worker will make the very best use of the implement he has persuaded the boss to buy. A worker with no enthusiasm eventually drifts away and perhaps, finding no outlet for his keen interest in some mechanical thing, will leave farming altogether. Five men in a hundred leave the field in a year, for one reason or another, and the town absorbs them when the rural community itself doesn't find them a satisfactory outlet.

Life on the land doesn't mean what it once meant – a poverty-line struggle for survival. The farmworker is paid less than his equivalent in town, if there is any labour equivalent to the man whose lot is cultivating and husbandry. His built-in benefits are probably not much better than those of his grandfather for the Victorian labourer would be provided with wood and coals, his potatoes and turnips, the rabbits he might snare or net, a row of whatever he planted for his master, a pig from the litter if he fattened them all to his master's satisfaction. A lot of these benefits have now been priced out of the bargain by virtue of the cost of feeding stuffs and the high market value of special blood strains. It boils down to the truth that a man who lives and works on the land must have something beyond just an aptitude for the work. He must love the environment, the sort of thing he has to do, and the freedom his work gives him, not to go off to a football match or a night with the bowling team, but to use his initiative, to experiment and even once in a while, make his own mistakes. When the boss consults him and asks his advice they are farming. When the boss rolls away in his new Volvo he is a different man, but it was always this way in his grandfather's day and if someone is entitled to his profit, when there is one, someone must stand the loss that is a part of the same precarious business.

A farmer loading his tractor to fodder
his moorland cattle

84

In impossible weather a farmer looks on while his dogs attempt to round up the stock ready for market

Gentleman farmer

Whereas at one time farmers could afford a good many hands, today's labour costs are beyond the reach of most. Years ago this particular hedge would have been properly laid, but the fence now provides a quick and easy solution to a time-consuming problem

As if in a scene from *Swan Lake*, a
farmer herds his cattle into a field

Old style haymaking where the field
proved too small to justify the expense
of hiring a baler

Many farms are still in the hands of
families who portion out the work and
profit between them, like these three
batchelor brothers in the Cotswolds

Cliff Waycott cleaning the Devonport leat on Dartmoor. These man-made waterways follow the contours of the land, diverting their water from streams. In Victorian times many were built to provide power in the wheelhouses of mines and factories. Surviving ones like this feed the reservoirs for the city

Farm sales attract farmers from all over the county, with the prospect of many good machines going at bargain prices

Sale ring at Hereford market where a horse is paraded before the eyes of prospective buyers

Potato harvest near the River Trent
where the crop, after being riddled and
graded, has been sacked by a team of
helpers

Tractor and tedder; this implement is used to shake up cut hay to prevent mould forming whilst it lies on the ground in damp conditions

# Animals and Husbandry

Without doubt the dog has kept company with man longer than any other animal, but lumbering alongside, or even following him like the dog itself, were oxen and sheep. Man rode the horse into battle and domesticated the wild pig and the fowl of the jungle. All of them are still there, living in association with the countryman in one way or another, exploited by him, taking up most of his waking hours, fascinating him and making his life richer.

The shepherd may not lead his sheep as his Mediterranean counterpart still does, but he lives most of his time in close proximity to the flock. He often has to move it to better pasture. He takes it out on the road, marshals it with his dogs, and keeps it on the move to the place where the grass is greener. His dogs are an extension of his body. Sometimes they have to be an extension of his mind and run in to prevent the sheep flowing away like water down a slope. The whole business harks back to the hunting of the wolfpack, but without the kill this kind of out-flanking movement was once intended to produce. The sheepdog slinks, darts, claps down and creeps forward on its belly. The leader of the pack is the old fellow with the crook who whistles, waves his arm, or simply gives a hand-signal to change the direction of movement, bring the flock to the dipping pen, the fold where they may be looked over, or the shearing place built of hurdles or bales of straw. The whole business is to exploit the sheep, an animal that crops the grass closer than a cow, and far less fastidiously than a horse! The sheep, poor beast, must give up its fleece and finally its flesh, bones and skin, but this is what the countless generations of breeding have been for.

The shepherd is no sentimentalist about the sheep or the dog: he couldn't survive without either of them. The sheepdog is no pet but a workmate. When he is a very good dog he may be specially trained for trials in which he will demonstrate his special talent, dogging sheep through hurdles and cutting one out from the rest. This particular breed of dog has changed over the centuries but the work of the shepherd is probably the least changed of all the branches of husbandry. Sheep can't be kept in a factory. They may be shorn of their wool by the use of electrical gear, but there is little else about their management that can be mechanized. The strange thing is that men still choose to be shepherds in a world in which everyone else looks for the easy way and the softer life.

The pig never quite took the imagination of man or pleased him quite so much as a domesticated animal. It is not so easily herded. Its way of getting its food is rough and ready. The countryman who keeps large herds of pigs is always a bit of an outcast because it is hard to keep the animal spotlessly clean. Unlike the sheep, however, the wretched pig can be kept in a factory, fed a special ration of food, swilled clean twice a day, and will live, a pink and healthy animal, under electric light with air-conditioning built into the vast shed in which such animals are usually kept. Until recent years the cottager kept a couple of pigs in the piggery behind his house, one to be cured and feed the family, and one to be sold to bring in a few pounds. All kinds of difficulties have been put in the way of the backyard pig-breeder or pig fattener, for few cottagers ever actually bred their own pig. The incidence of swine fever, more stringent health regulations, and the requirement that swill had to be processed before it could be fed, put paid to the cottager's pig. Here and there, however, someone with the good luck to have the room, a field in which a pig might root, the right kind of food and the means of boiling it up, still keeps the old-fashioned, free-ranging pig that never will know air-conditioning or barley ration, and happily roots in the shade of oak or beech tree.

Goats that browse on their hind legs to trim a hedge or keep a green tidy are still loved by country people who have the time and inclination to sit in at a milking platform and milk the animal. Goats' milk, and the cheese made from it, are highly nutritious by-products of the goat's lawn-mowing ability. A family of geese will fill the same purpose, though the Michaelmas goose has tended to go out of fashion. Geese are not so easily divested of their feathers and down as turkeys are. They tend to be fatty and the day of using goose grease on one's chest to keep out the winter cold has long gone. The countryman keeps the goose as a watchdog – geese were the watchdogs of Rome – because he has a taste for the rich meat, or simply because he loves the sight of them. Four geese will crop as much grass as a sheep, they say, but they are extraordinarily dignified birds and beautiful. Ducks too, seem to please the eye as much as geese. A pond or a stream that runs close by a dwelling isn't really right without its domestic duck, an Indian Runner perhaps, a Khaki Campbell, a couple of snow-white Aylesburys, even the Muscovy, the Mandarin or the Carolina, may swim through the muddied water or roost on the gravel strand.

The backyard hen hasn't the colourful image of the waterbird, but she provides the breakfast egg and, where the desire to have hens goes beyond the product, the bantam comes into its own. Hundreds of cottagers and small farmers keep bantams which will roost in the hedge or the orchard trees, lay away in the undergrowth or on the hay at the top of the barn. The bantam cocks will crow throughout the day and half the night, pleasing only the man who loves the sight of these jaunty dwarf chickens. Being closer to the hardy strain of jungle fowl, the bantam is a natural survivor. It gets by with a minimum of food concentrate, thriving on kitchen waste, potato peelings, bread and greenstuff.

The horse, however, is almost a self-indulgence on the part of the owner, for it is only rarely a working animal these days. The workhorse has long gone over the hill, though Shires, Clydesdales and other once famous breeds of draught-horses are still bred for show. The countryman's affection for the horse often exceeds his affection for the dog. The horse being a larger animal, is fortunately one that may be kept with less need for daily attention than a dog, or a collection of ducks and hens, so long as the weather is good and there is a plentiful supply of grass and a source of clean drinking water. Where the countryman is blessed with these things he can have his pony, providing it with oats, hay, and a little straw for bedding when it is stabled in the hard days of mid-winter. The sort of horse varies almost as much as the man who keeps it. It may be a hearty cob, a shaggy Shetland pony, a graceful hunter, a jumper, even a fast trotter. It will live to a considerable age and respond to gentle treatment, and above all it will have its own particular character. This is probably what makes the horse so attractive. It may take an experienced shepherd to know the faces of a flock of sheep and identify one from another, but the horse is uncannily like man in its variety of moods and the quirks of its nature. It co-operates with man. It is persuaded to do what he wants when he has the patience to work at it.

Two other animals featuring in the life of the countryman are the hound and the dog, neither classified as workers though the countryman expects more of his dog than the townsman. He looks to it to root out the rat that lives under the henhouse, mark a rabbit in the hedge, flush a pheasant from the gorse or bracken, give him warning when someone, or some animal, is trespassing on his property, or mind his car when he is in the market haggling with a dealer. This kind of dog wouldn't herd sheep and would stampede the milking cow on her way into the shippon, but he generally has a little bit of the sheepdog and the cow-herding dog in him, a touch of the spaniel and the labrador, a trace of the whippet or the greyhound. He is fierce if he is chained, and sometimes he needs to be to keep thieves away from farm buildings and outhouses.  Such a dog has something of a guilt complex when taken through the wood. He knows what poaching is. He is sometimes a thief by nature, and occasionally even a trained thief. Unobtrusive, he waits on his master at the pub door, or huddles under the form his master is sitting on until enough talk has been talked and enough beer drunk to satisfy the most garrulous and the most thirsty of men. W. H. Hudson, the naturalist, recognized this dog, calling him 'the red dog', but that was simply because he had to have some colour. He certainly had no distinct shape or size, and his progeny are to be found everywhere throughout the length and breadth of the land.

The hound, of course, is a very different creature, a rather well-bred animal whose freedom, on those occasions when he is brought from behind the iron bars of the kennel, always makes him seem like a boisterous, over-excited schoolboy. He has been bred for his bone and stamina and he has a rather grand name. He has the habit of posing with other members of the pack and looks like an aristocrat which, if blood lines are anything to do with it, he really is. Hounds have family trees that rival those of their most illustrious owners. If they didn't come over with William the Conqueror it was because the people on the other side of the channel were reluctant to part with any of the great hunting hounds they bred. Foxhounds, beagles and bassets invariably have distinguished French ancestors.

Saddest of all the domesticated animals, however, is the poor cow. She is a milk producer and a beef producer. We turn her newly-born calf into veal. Her sturdy son is castrated to be herded into the barley beef factory, and no one cares. The story would bring tears to the eyes of the compassionate who might overlook the fact that we eat a great amount of beef, even at its present day price, and we certainly couldn't get through without milk and milk products which supply a great part of the protein and the minerals our bodies need. This is something a little remote from the cow on the meadow, an animal the townsman really doesn't associate with t-bone or sirloin, or even the pint on his doorstep. Milk comes from the bottle and not from the cow. The steak comes from the kitchen. Out on the green grass of the fenland, the marsh, the rich dairy country of Devon, Carmarthenshire and many other parts of the country, the cow feeds on herbage, ruminates and converts it into meat and milk. It is no longer a beast of burden, the companion of the carter or the ploughman, but purely and simply a kind of converter of hay and swede, whose input and output are continually monitored. The countryman has never been too enthusiastic about it as a species of animal, which is doubly sad.

'The dog has kept company with man
longer than any other animal'

There is more to moving a flock of sheep than just driving them frantically into a corner. The shepherd moves up with caution and his dog remains ready to cut off any member of the flock that might rush back

His temper rising, this farmer does it the
hard way without the aid of a dog

The brood sow adopts a typically
defensive stance as she pauses while
conveying her litter along the mountain
road

There are a number of ways of catching
a duck and a fisherman's landing net is
usually the favourite but this old lady
achieves her purpose with a salmon
tailer

At the onset of the drought a moorland
pony with her foal comes down to the
falling water-line of a favourite drinking
place

The remnants of a barrel kennel serve as a shelter for this chained dog as he guards the farmyard. Unlike the town pet, farmers' dogs tend not to be pampered

A pack of hounds waits in anticipation
for the master to have done with the
formalities and for the huntsman to lead
them away

Tired of his enforced isolation, an
amorous bull bellows to a neighbour's
cattle

A brock-faced cow with a fine set of
horns looks curiously over the garden
wall of an abandoned farm. Most
farmers these days would dehorn such
an animal

# Transport

The business of getting about for the man who lives in the remote countryside is a problem that simply has to be solved. The world is disinclined to come to his door with all the things he needs. He must travel by one means of transport or another. His great grandfather did it on foot or on horseback. The penny farthing bicycle and the original boneshaker weren't ideal for steep hills and the man who could keep a pony moved what he had to move on its back or in a cart or gig. The declining rural population has never been able to support an economic service of any kind. Railway branch lines came only as far as the prospect of a profit would bring them. The carrier's cart travelled the old coach roads and linked villages beyond the main arteries of communication. The horsebus plied between small towns and cities in the main. Unless the countryman provided his own means of transport he stayed where he was and vegetated. Even in the remote villages in wilder parts of the country there are still a few old people who have only visited a large town once in their lives. Here and there, there are people who have never seen the sea. Their fathers and mothers had been content with the world as they found it and never thought for a minute that on the other side of the hill the grass might be greener.

The railway system was probably the main hope of staying the depopulation of the countryside so long as people who lost their living on the land through steadily increasing use of machinery could travel in to places where there was industry. The inexorable encroachment of the machine on the manual labourer's field made the railway system less and less profitable as young people were forced to move to the town. There were fewer people out at the end of the branch line to whom goods could be sold. The farmers were still there, of course, and people who made a living by providing an essential service of one sort or another, but the internal combustion engine, developed in Victorian times and finally employed on the land, spelt the beginning of a new era in which the workhorse would be redundant and with it, a great many people whose livelihood had been adjusted merely to horsepower. The workhorse has gone. The motorcar reigns supreme. Only the old-fashioned countryman keeps a pony and uses a cart. The winds and elbows have been taken out of the country roads and they have been redesigned for much faster traffic.

Even in this high speed world the countryman doesn't always compromise. He travels on occasion in a gig, with a horse-drawn barrow and on a bicycle. The bicycle often belonged to his old dad. It rattles and creaks and it carries as much as the old donkey when it is wheeled along, loaded with a bag of swedes or potatoes, a crate of chickens or a sack of oats slumped on the crossbar. Whatever else he may be, the countryman isn't self-conscious about the way he travels. Distance is the great thing for consuming a man's time and when he wants to get to the cheapjack's market to buy a roll of floor covering, or some pots and pans for his wife he will travel by whatever means are to hand, the battered van or even the tractor. Everyone travels the best way he can and tries to forget the miles between his cottage and the fair, the circus or the farm sale. There is no help for it.

There was until recent years a reasonable bus service beyond the railway system. When the branch line of the railway closed it seemed that the bus service would take the railway's place everywhere. Out in the hinterland, however, the bus ran for fewer and fewer passengers, trundled up the byways and through the back lanes to little villages where no one got on and no one got off. The system began to die at the tip of the tree. In the larger villages people complained that the bus didn't run as often as before. The service was getting worse. Fares were going up. Where the bus had come and gone once in the morning and once in the afternoon it began to come once a day, once every other day, once a week. The people of the countryside who wanted to get into town to suit their immediate needs found alternative means. Those who had the money bought old cars and never used the twice-a-week bus again. This in its turn made the bus service even more uneconomic and the die was cast in the end when the price of petrol and oil rocketed.

Where could a man avoid such a serious drain on his pocket? Nowhere but in the town itself. The town had been creeping out to swallow the village. Now the rural population begins to move into town faster than it ever did before. People who aren't wanted on the land move into town because there never will be employment for them out there, either on the harvest field or the cattle pasture. No one needs hedgers and ditchers, ploughmen or milkers any more. Even the molecatcher is redundant and moves out.

What has really happened is complicated by the fact that the markets, once the lifeblood of farming, are no longer thriving in small towns. Business has moved away. The prime beef of the pasture can be whirled off down the motorway to some distant Smithfield, some abattoir in France, Italy or Germany. The small country market town tends to lose its importance with the passing of the years. Fifty years ago there were fewer cattle transports and no great motorways along which stock could be quickly taken to the other end of the country. Often the bullocks walked the road to market and the sheep too, were driven to the 'back end' sale along the road, with sheepdogs and shepherds in attendance.

The road cattle transport system evolved in the same way as inward road haulage bringing goods into the country, not to a siding as the railway system had done, but right to the door of the farmer who had ordered them, saving him a day or more when he would have had to use men and transport to bring the stuff from the depot to his farm-yard. The three-decked sheep transport comes to the farm. The sheep are quickly driven up the ramp and enclosed. The farmer goes back to his daily routine, or to watch his television, and the thing is done with.

The same thing happens whether he wants to get rid of sheep or bull calves, pigs or bullocks. The roads are there for rapid transportation of things. An articulated truck brings him all the fertiliser he will need in a year. A grain drier comes along the same road. A tanker rolls up with fuel for the machinery. The farmer himself is in and out of the market on the far side of his county before the morning is gone, and walking his field to see what the machine has been doing in the afternoon. Few people travel aimlessly along the lanes of the countryside now except the tourist and the sightseer. Everyone is on the move. It used to be a disgrace to lie in bed when the sun was up and the corn ready for cutting. Now it is a disgrace to hang about looking over hedges and admiring the scenery.

Even the children of the countryside are travellers because times have changed for school children too. The rural school has closed down. It never was the perfect way of teaching even the three r's for the country schoolmaster had to cope with children of all ages from five to fourteen. If he had thirty or forty boys and girls he had more than he could ever hope to manage. It hadn't mattered when these children were to be potato-pickers and bird-scarers waiting for a more adult job that really didn't require them to be able to read or write. Then mechanical revolution took away the opportunity to work in the field at tying sheaves by hand, stooking and rick-building, and the reduction in the juvenile population made the country schoolmaster redundant.

The village school was hardly better placed, even when it had a staff of four or five teachers. The educational requirement was a much higher one than the small village school could meet. The school had to be gathered in to the town and the children conveyed to the secondary or grammar school there. Now a school bus makes a daily round gathering up country children and transporting them to town. The service is, in fact, a much more reliable one than their parents still have available to them if they are compelled to travel by bus. Happily a new sort of transport is at present taking the place of the diminishing country bus service — the mini-bus. This is a private enterprise or co-operative effort to meet the needs of people who can't afford to run a car and pay tribute to the oil barons.

There is no turning back, however. The day of the horse is gone for good. No one can stay in business going back to the pace of the Victorians. The roads are for speed and ease of transportation. The ox wagon, the stage coach, the four-in-hand belong in the dim days of centuries past. Taking his time ploughing a field the farmer faces ruin. Taking his time getting livestock to the market he will run into the red. Taking his time getting from his village to his work at the creamery or the agricultural depot the worker will get the sack! Walking to school the country boy will never get his O levels and be able to move away from the wilderness to the bright lights of town, and the fat wage packet he might one day have working on that production line.

Change, however, is never overnight and hardly ever complete in a lifetime. Just as here and there mills still grind the season's crop of wheat, and blacksmiths shoe a shire horse there are people who hold to the old way and travel slowly, hopefully, being passed by a hurrying world that less than a century ago went at the same pace. A great many country people wave and take off their hats to them as they sail past. That both are expressing their feeling about what matters in life never occurs to either. There were always those who preferred to take their time and always those who were in a hurry.

Open highland dictates the situation of this huddled farm enclosed by drystone walls. The trees, planted against the prevailing wind, provide shelter from frequent gales

Railway enthusiasts busy checking
levels of newly-laid track. Ripped up in
the early 60s, the line is now being
restored, and the rolling stock
reconditioned for the benefit of tourists

A grocer on his rounds transports his
produce on a home-made cart fashioned
from a car's back axle and wheels,
with two steel pipes as makeshift
shafts

Farmer's wife out for a Sunday morning drive on a modern version of a horse-drawn pole yoke for two ponies

On the way home from the shops, one
mother solves the problem of keeping
the children in order and spreading the
load

Looking like a stage entrance stopped
in its tracks, a tractor sits between
tattered drapes

This steam-roller is said to be one of the
last in use by a local authority anywhere
in Britain, and the driver, being proud
of the fact, maintains it in perfect
condition

POWYS C.C. · HIGHWAYS·

RADNORSHIRE
COUNTY COUNCIL

Sports day at a Cotswold village school. There are now fewer of these rural schools still surviving as a result of government policy to centralise education

The village still needs to go from here to
there, and the mini-bus, often run by
locals, replaces a service that larger
companies found uneconomic